PROPERTY OF
GRIFFIN
FREE PUBLIC LIB
Auburn, New Hamp
MW01675982
Griffin Free Public Librar
89952

Lady Adrian

by Amy Bryson

Phyllis Giroux, Illustrator

PCB Publishing
Derry, New Hampshire
Printed in Singapore

Copyright © 2002 by PCB Publishing

All rights reserved. No part of this book may be reproduced or transmitted in any form or by any means, electronic or mechanical, including photo-copying, recording, or by any information storage and retrieval system, without permission in writing from the publisher.

Published by PCB Publishing
Derry, New Hampshire 03038

Publisher's Cataloging-in Publication Data
Bryson, Amy.
Lady Adrian / Amy Bryson. —Derry, NH:
PCB Publishing, 2002.
p. cm.
ISBN 0-9711093-0-3
1. Ladybugs—Juvenile fiction. I. Title.

PZ10.3/.B797/La	2002	2001-095254
[E]	— dc21	CIP

PROJECT COORDINATION BY JENKINS GROUP, INC.
COVER AND BOOK DESIGN BY THERESA BAEHR

06 05 04 03 02 • 6 5 4 3 2

Printed in Singapore

This book is dedicated to my niece, Adrian.
For the happiness you have brought to the family,
Especially to your Mom and Dad.
-I Love you

For my Daughter Paige,
My true inspiration
And to all of my Nieces and Nephews,
May the sweetness of this rhyme
Carry you a lifetime.

Sincere thanks to my family for all their love, and support.
Heartfelt thanks to my husband Sean, who encouraged me throughout,
and a Special thanks to my grandmother Phyllis
for the beautiful
Way she brought my text to life.
I love you all so very much.

In Loving memory of
Paula Harvey

 Once upon a time, in the beautiful land of ladybugs, there lived the sweetest little bug named Adrian.

Adrian is the youngest of five most adorable Ladies and four very handsome Lads.

She has brought such happiness to the family, especially to her mom and dad.

Sweet Adrian grew and grew. 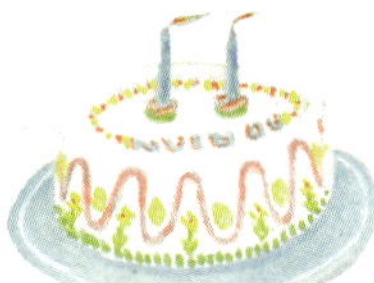 She had her second birthday, and now she was two!

Now Adrian, with bigger wings  and a few more spots, began having lady-like thoughts. Adrian asked herself,

"If I pay close attention to what the others say and do could I become a lady? Could this be true?"

Adrian listened and heard the others say, "please" whenever they would ask for something.

Whenever they were given something (like a piggyback ride)  she always heard them say, "Thank You."

Adrian thought these words sounded very nice and she wanted to say them, too!

Still paying close attention, Adrian noticed that whenever the ladies and lads saw one another they would smile and say "Hello." And if Mom needed to remind them, they never in a naughty voice said, "NO!" Adrian thought this was so nice and she wanted to do it, too.

Adrian also noticed that they played so well...  *Is it because they Share?*

If I too share like them, would they let me play... could this be true?

I'll try it, thought Adrian. "Playing is sharing" is what I've always been told.

I suppose if I try it, then I'll know.

One more thing Adrian  saw them do.

They covered their mouths when they

sneezed or coughed, then they said, "Excuse Me" to top it off!

Adrian thought, with her finger resting on her chin, I can remember to do these things. "Please" and "Thank You" for everyone, and big smiles when I say "Hello" to friends. Sharing when playing is important to know, and never, never sounding naughty when I say the word "NO." Oh- and one more thing to top it off, I'll always cover my mouth when I sneeze or cough!

Adrian had become so grown up and lady-like.
She made her family very proud. Adrian was SO polite
and SO well behaved, her mom and dad knew that they
could take her anywhere in the beautiful land of ladybugs.

All the other ladies and lads looked forward to playing with Adrian because she shared so well. Everyone thought that little Adrian would grow up to be Princess Lady Adrian of all the land of ladybugs.

Sure enough,  with all Adrian's nice manners and good behavior, she did just that!